ATHENS

THE CITY AT A GLANCE

GW00683799

Monastiraki Square
Between the old part of the c[...]
Psyrri, this square is home t[...]
Buy souvenirs in the shops a[...]
street merchants, and try a [...]

Tower of the Winds
In the Roman Agora site, th[...]
tower (each side representin[...]
built by the astronomer Andronicus in
the first century BC. There was once a water
clock inside and sundials on the exterior.
Roman Forum, Markou Avriliou

Athinas Street
Connecting Monastiraki to Omonia, this busy
road is home to Athens' Central Market –
the meat, fish, vegetables and spices give off
quite an aroma – as well as Kotzia Square
(see p074), overlooked by the Town Hall.

Omonia Square
A recent redesign of the square failed to live
up to expectations. It's now a central meeting
point, but not a particularly welcoming one.

Ermou Street
One of Athens' most popular shopping areas.
You can find everything here, and the street
performers add a nice touch.

Parliament/Syntagma Square
This legendary square has witnessed much
of the city's history. The dominant presence
is the Parliament building, but historic hotels
also underline the links to the past.

Athens Cathedral
This Greek Orthodox Church, finished in 1862,
has undergone many changes over the years,
which is probably why it lacks a true style.
Mitropoleos Square

INTRODUCTION
THE CHANGING FACE OF THE URBAN SCENE

Few cities in the world are as loaded with history as Athens. Acting as both a magnet for visitors and a reason for the Greeks to take pride in the continuity of their culture, the evocative remains of the ancient city-state can still be seen, rising up like islands from today's rather chaotic urban environment. And while Athens may appear blighted by unchecked development, there are, thankfully, some appealing touches of modernism scattered around. The city is an unsystematic mix of old and new, of west and east; a site of constructions, reconstructions, renovations and a few innovations (the 2004 Olympics worked wonders on that score).

There's no rivalry: antithesis, maybe; coexistence, yes. Athens is a densely populated European capital, which clings to its past but is also increasingly multicultural. You wouldn't describe it as a global city – at least, not yet – but it's getting there. Stylish bars, restaurants, clubs, galleries, concert halls and malls can be found rubbing up against traditional Greek attractions, such as bouzouki music, *souvlaki* and *frappé* (chilled coffee). In order to get to grips with Athens, it's advisable to do a lot of walking, taking in everything from shiny Pentelikon marble in the Acropolis and the little streets of Plaka to mirror-windowed office buildings and ugly TV aerials. It's the best way to discover the true aesthetics (as in the Greek *aisthanomai* – to perceive properly, using the senses) of a restless, sometimes tiring, but always diverting city.

ESSENTIAL INFO

FACTS, FIGURES AND USEFUL ADDRESSES

TOURIST OFFICE
Greek Tourist Office
26 Vasilissis Amalias
T 210 331 0716
www.gnto.gr

TRANSPORT
Athens Metro
www.ametro.gr
Car hire
Avis
T 210 353 0578
Hertz
T 210 922 0102
Taxi
Ikaros
T 210 515 2800
Thermal Buses
T 185
www.ethel.gr

EMERGENCY SERVICES
Ambulance
T 166
Fire
T 199
Police
T 100
24-hour pharmacy
Bacacos
3 Agiou Konstantinou
T 210 523 2631

EMBASSIES
British Embassy
1 Ploutarhou
T 210 727 2600
www.british-embassy.gr
US Embassy
91 Vasilissis Sophias
T 210 721 2951
athens.usembassy.gov

MONEY
American Express
318 Messogion
T 210 659 0700
travel.americanexpress.com

POSTAL SERVICES
Post Office
Syntagma Square
T 210 323 7573
Shipping
UPS
T 210 614 6510
www.ups.com

BOOKS
Athens: A Guide to Recent Architecture
by Errica Protestou (Ellipsis Arts)
Lysistrata and Other Plays by
Aristophanes (Penguin Classics)
The Republic by Plato (Penguin Classics)

WEBSITES
Architecture
www.culture2000.tee.gr
Art/Design
www.culture.gr
Newspapers
www.athensnews.gr

COST OF LIVING
**Taxi from Eleftherios Venizelos
Airport to city centre**
€29
Cappuccino
€3.90
Packet of cigarettes
€3
Daily newspaper
€2
Bottle of champagne
€80

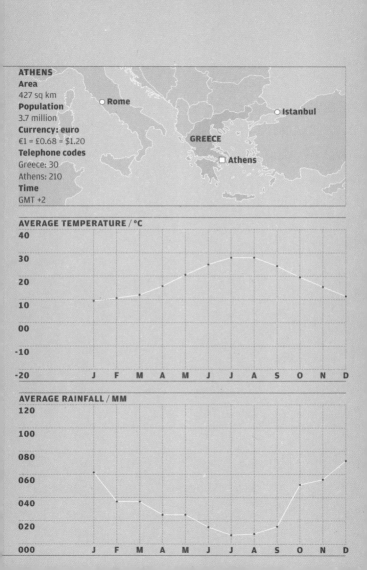

ATHENS

Area
427 sq km
Population
3.7 million
Currency: euro
€1 = £0.68 = $1.20
Telephone codes
Greece: 30
Athens: 210
Time
GMT +2

Rome

Istanbul

GREECE

Athens

AVERAGE TEMPERATURE / °C

| 40 |
| 30 |
| 20 |
| 10 |
| 00 |
| -10 |
| -20 |

J F M A M J J A S O N D

AVERAGE RAINFALL / MM

| 120 |
| 100 |
| 080 |
| 060 |
| 040 |
| 020 |
| 000 |

J F M A M J J A S O N D

NEIGHBOURHOODS

THE AREAS YOU NEED TO KNOW AND WHY

To help you navigate the city, we've chosen the most interesting districts (see the map inside the back cover) and underlined featured venues in colour, according to their location (see below); those venues that are outside these areas are not coloured.

PLAKA, THISSIO AND MONASTIRAKI

Pedestrianisation has given this historic part of the city a more relaxed character. Take a traffic-free stroll through ancient Athens' remains, from the Acropolis to the tiny shops of Plaka (the old city), and the buzzy bars of Thissio. In Monastiraki, stop for coffee on Adhrianou and enjoy the excellent views of the Agora. Located just behind here in Avissynias Square is the popular and busy flea market.

PSYRRI AND GAZI

Calm during the daytime, but extremely lively at night, both of these formerly down-at-heel neighbourhoods have been transformed in recent years. Psyrri's eating and drinking options range from small tavernas with live Greek music to cute bars and clubs. Gazi is charming on summer evenings: choose between rooftop bars with views of the beautifully lit Technopolis (see p010) and tiny venues serving refreshing cocktails.

NORTHERN SUBURBS

The greener part of the city, where the rich once spent their summer holidays, is now an unquestionably urban space, full of big offices and department stores. But it's still a locus of status and glamour, with plenty of designer boutiques to match. Actually, this applies mostly to Kifissia and part of Maroussi, where OAKA, the Olympic Park (see p094), is located. Chalandri is quite commercial, but far more laid-back.

SOUTHERN SUBURBS

These suburbs share their coastline, and the fun, with Athens' summer hot spots. In Pireas, particularly in Mikrolimano, tavernas, bars and restaurants next to the ocean serve fresh seafood and, of course, ouzo. Paleo Faliro and Kalamaki have their charming promenades, Glifada is packed with bars and cafés, and Vouliagmeni has sandy beaches, which make a great escape from the heat of the city.

SYNTAGMA AND KOLONAKI

Syntagma is famous for the high-camp Changing of the Guard outside the Hellenic Parliament (T 210 370 7000). Here you will also find many of the city's museums, embassies and, on Panepistimiou, its Neoclassical Trilogy: the University of Athens (www.uoa.gr), the Athens Academy (see p013) and the National Library (T 210 338 2541). Kolonaki remains a chic shopping area, although recently it has developed a more easy-going feel.

PANGRATI AND AMPELOKIPOI

Pangrati is home to the Panathenaic Stadium (see p014), where the first modern Olympics were held in 1896. A few streets away is the National Gallery (T 210 723 5857). Vasilissis Sofias, an avenue linking Syntagma Square with Ampelokipoi, boasts the Athens Concert Hall, Megaron (T 210 728 2333), Museum of Cycladic Art (see p087) and Walter Gropius' modernist American Embassy (T 210 721 2951).

LANDMARKS
THE SHAPE OF THE CITY SKYLINE

With buildings spanning millennia and a rather casual approach to urban planning, Athens seems more of a haphazard collage than a unified work of art. As a result, it is difficult to think of the city as a single entity. The outlying suburbs are growing fast, yet the historic core acts as a powerfully symbolic focal point, with, of course, the Parthenon in the Acropolis at its heart. Athenians love their myths; they rarely climb their 'holy rock', but the cafés in Monastiraki and Plaka below are packed all day.

Go for a walk in the Ancient Agora and the Roman Agora, and discover the octagonal Tower of Winds, built by the astronomer Andronicus around 100-50BC. Also within the traditional centre are the Theatre of Dionysus and the Odeon of Herodes Atticus (Dhionysiou Areopayitou); the latter, built by the Roman governor in 161AD, was reclad with marble in the 1950s and is once more a functioning amphitheatre. The Temple of Hephaestus, dating from 449BC, is the best-preserved classical temple in Greece.

The modern state is represented by the neoclassicism of the Parliament building facing Syntagma Square, Athens Academy (see p013) and Zappeion Hall (see p012). For industrial chic, head to the Technopolis (overleaf), a former gasworks that has found new life as a cultural centre. Lastly, relax on Posidonos Avenue, a waterfront promenade where the locals take in the sea air.
For full addresses, see Resources.

Technopolis
Built for the French Gas Company in
1862, this former factory is known by
locals as 'Gazi'. It suspended operations
in 1984, but is now fully restored as an
industrial museum and cultural centre,
hosting concerts and art exhibitions.
At night, its beautifully lit chimneys are
a beacon for the stylish restaurants and
bars of the surrounding Gazi district.
100 Pireos, T 210 346 0981

Zappeion Hall and Gardens

Sadly, uneven urban development has led to a city with a pronounced lack of green spaces, so don't leave Athens without a stroll in the tree-lined Zappeion Gardens (adjoining the National Gardens). Then switch your focus to Zappeion Hall (above), an imposing neoclassical building designed by Danish architect Theophilus Hansen for the 1896 Olympics. Completed in 1888, the hall has hosted key moments in Greek history, such as the accession of Greece to the EEC in 1979. Stop for a coffee and a snack in the open-air Lallabai Lounge (in Aigli Zappio), then make your way to the nearby Hadrian's Arch, which is made of white Pentelikon marble. *Vasilissis Amalias, T 210 323 7602, www.zappeion.gr*

Athens Academy

Part of the city's so-called Neoclassical Trilogy, which includes the University of Athens (completed in 1864) and the National Library (built in 1902), Athens Academy is considered one of the most beautiful examples of the style. Designed by Theophilus Hansen, who borrowed elements from the Erechtheion, and supervised by Ernst Ziller, it was completed in 1902. The hexastyle portico, with a pediment sculpted by Leonidas Drosis, leads to a unique reading room decorated with Ionic columns. Drosis also sculpted the monumental columns of Athena, goddess of wisdom, and Apollo, god of light, as well as the statues of Plato and Socrates in front of the building.
28-32 Panepistimiou, T 210 360 0207

Panathenaic Stadium

This marble structure stands on the site of the original stadium built by the orator Lycurgus in 330-329BC, in order to host the Panathenaic Games; Herodes Atticus restored it in the second century AD and it was rebuilt to host the first Olympics of modern times, in 1896. New venues stole the show for the 2004 Games, but the archery final was held here.

Vasileos Konstantinou

HOTELS

WHERE TO STAY AND WHICH ROOMS TO BOOK

The 2004 Olympic Games gave the Athenian hotel industry an opportunity to reinvent itself, with some extensive renovations and interesting newcomers. So now you have it all: ultra-modern design at Semiramis (see p037) and Fresh (see p022); fashionable boutique-style hotels in Ochre & Brown (see p018), Periscope (see p026), Eridanus (78 Pireos, T 210 520 5360) and Baby Grand (see p028), and old-fashioned luxury at the Grande Bretagne (see p034) and Pentelikon (66 Dheliyianni, T 210 623 0650). All of these have greatly improved facilities and service, in order to cater to the needs of both business and leisure travellers. When it comes to rest and relaxation, the hotels in the leafy northern suburbs, such as Life Gallery (see p024), have to compete with those in the luxurious seaside resorts, such as the Astir Palace (see p019), Grechotel Cape Sounio (see p098) and Grand Resort Lagonissi (see p032); for the latter two it's best to hire a car.

Even if you haven't got a room, that's no reason to miss out on the hotels' glamorous bars, which serve some of the best cocktails in town. Try the classy Alexander Bar in the Grand Bretagne, the designer Semiramis bar and the new wine bar at Life Gallery. In-house hotel restaurants can vary from the indifferent to the gastronomically superb, notably Vardis in the Pentelikon and Kohylia in the Grand Resort Lagonissi – so choose carefully.
For full addresses and room rates, see Resources.

Twentyone

Everything here revolves around the age at which you 'get the key to the door'. Located at 21 Kolokotroni, Twentyone has, you guessed it, 21 rooms: 16 Superior Rooms and five Loft Suites with skylights, where you can lie on your bed and look at the stars. The design is contemporary (mostly monochrome, with red accents) and is based on functionality. The walls, however, are a highlight. A local artist,

Georgia Sagri, has used them as a canvas for her semi-serious, crayon-like works, which give the rooms and the lobby (above) a hip, art-gallery aura.
21 Kolokotroni/Mykonou, T 210 623 3521, www.twentyone.gr

Ochre & Brown

A recent arrival in the city centre, Ochre & Brown is a small-scale hotel with just 10 comfortable rooms and one suite. All are decorated in earthy tones, with hints of more vivid colours that seem to underline the warm, relaxing atmosphere, as in the lobby (above). Elegant and modern, with tasteful details and marble bathrooms, the interior is extremely cosy and you can't beat the view of the Acropolis from Junior Suite's balcony. Located at the heart of the city's nightlife, Ochre & Brown has a charming Lounge Bar that also serves Mediterranean-influenced dishes.
7 Leokoriou, T 210 331 2950,
www.ochreandbrown.com

Astir Palace

This complex consists of three five-star hotels: The Westin and Arion Resort & Spa, both recently renovated, and the Aphrodite Hotel, due to reopen in 2008 as a W hotel. They share a pine-dotted private peninsula, with three beaches and views of the Saronic Gulf. Arion has elegant dining rooms and 123 generously sized bedrooms, all tastefully furnished in earth tones. The Westin has 162 rooms and suites, such as the Ambassador (above), decorated in soothing colours with modern artwork, and a striking modernist lobby (overleaf). Tennis courts, a pool and the Glifada golf course will appeal to sporty types.

40 Apollonos, Vouliagmeni, T 210 890 2000, www.astir-palace.gr

Lobby, The Westin

Fresh

A bright, pink glass reception area (right) provides a vibrant introduction to this cheerful hotel. Minimalist lines combine with comfort, pop furniture and vivid colours to give the public areas and all 133 rooms, including the Executive Rooms (above) and suites a playful air. Suite 707 is our favourite, for its curvaceous bath situated inside the room. The hotel also provides a gym, steam bath and sauna to help you relax. You might need them. Fresh adds a contemporary edge to the buzzy, multicultural neighbourhood where it is located, which includes the central market, and is close to Psyrri's clubs and bars. Have a light supper at the ninth-floor Air Lounge Pool Bar, then margaritas at the Orange Bar, which takes its name from the vivid slab of Corian running through its centre.
26 Sophokleous/Klisthenous,
T 210 524 8511, www.freshhotel.gr

Life Gallery

Surrounded by cedars and pine trees, this hotel has two buildings, the main one (right) dating from the early 1970s. But don't expect retro surroundings; a restoration has given Life Gallery a contemporary face. Wood, glass and steel underline the minimalist interior design, while elegant furniture (by Gervasoni, Interni, Minotti, Casa Milano, Kasthall and Armani Casa) and works by contemporary Greek artists (Lapas, Takis, Kessanlis) add to the aesthetics. Simplicity is the main idea, with the addition of high-tech touches in the 30 rooms, such as the Superior (above), which all feature a balcony/atrium area. The combination of sleek lines and comfort continues in the public areas, particularly the two pools and Ananea Spa and Gym, as well as the new Wine Gallery Restaurant and Bar. *103 Leoforos Thisseos, T 210 626 0400, www.bluegr.com*

Periscope

Functional with a futuristic twist, this hotel was designed by Deca Architects. The 22 rooms, including the four Junior Suites (above), are decorated mostly in grey with hints of blue, black and red. They feature a fair sprinkling of art and design details, and aren't exactly what you would call cosy — they're more like stylish bachelor pads. The Penthouse Suite steals the show, with its jacuzzi (left) on the roof and panoramic view of Athens. Even if you're not staying here, call in to take a visual tour around the city using the eponymous periscope in the lounge.
22 Haritos, T 210 729 7200,
www.periscope.gr

Baby Grand

Located bang in the city centre, this boutique hotel features a lively décor: many of its 68 rooms (there are also 11 suites), such as the Deluxe (above), have graffiti-style patterns painted on the walls. Inspired by Japanese paintings, comic culture, Byzantine iconography and art nouveau, each of the Baby Grand's rooms has a unique ambience; sadly, the rest of the hotel is not quite as inventive.

However, the ground-floor restaurant, Meat Me, is, as its name suggests, absolute heaven for carnivores.
65 Athinas/Lykourgou, T 210 325 0900, www.grecotel.gr

St George Lycabettus

Although it has undergone numerous redesigns since its opening in 1974 — it was last revamped in 2003 — and leans more towards a contemporary aesthetic, this hotel also gives a nod to the past, with, for example, its leather couches and marble surfaces. Still, the view of the Acropolis and Lycabettus Hill remains its high point. And with 154 rooms, decorated in styles which range from neoclassical to modern, such as the Marie Cristine Suite (right), it caters to most tastes. Just choose your view (we vote for the Acropolis) and preferred style of interior. The rest of the facilities will also tempt you, including the rooftop swimming pool (above) and the recently opened well-equipped spa and gym. Enjoy cocktails in the Sky Bar or Frame before dinner in Le Grand Balcon restaurant. *2 Kleomenous, T 210 729 0711, www.sglycabettus.gr*

Grand Resort Lagonissi

Set in 72 acres on a lush green peninsula, the Lagonissi's various suites, villas and bungalows all have views of the Aegean Sea. In the rooms, stone, oak and marble are the dominant materials, while the spacious, discreetly luxurious suites, such as the Dream (above), which has its own skylight, are decorated in soothing colours to match the ambience of their private veranda decks and heated pools overlooking the sea. Visit the Blu Spa for some serious pampering with ESPA products, and the resort's restaurants, to make the most of the seaside setting; our favourite is Kohylia.

40km Athens-Sounio, Lagonissi, T 229 107 6000, www.grandresort.gr

Grande Bretagne

This grande dame of the hotel scene is as opulent as they come. It opened its doors in 1874, and has numbered among its guests politicians, celebrities and business tycoons, from Churchill and the Kennedys to Maria Callas; at the same time it has hosted Athens' most significant social and political gatherings. Some of its features inevitably faded with time, but the 2000 renovation restored the hotel to its original glory, for instance in the Royal Suite bathroom (right). French and Italian neoclassical furniture, silk draperies and artworks are to be found in its 290 rooms and 31 suites. The winter garden, with a stained-glass ceiling, is exquisite, while the Alexander Bar is a favourite among politicians. The hotel's elegant restaurant, GB Corner, has a roof garden with an uninterrupted view of the Acropolis. *Constitution Square, T 210 333 0000, www.grandebretagne.gr*

The Margi

Despite the fact that it's located in the southern suburb of Vouliagmeni, the revamped Margi feels more like a city-centre establishment. The colonial-style décor is charming, especially in the public areas, and features warm colours with eclectic furniture. There are 88 intimate but sufficiently sized rooms, some of which overlook the pool, others the mountain or the sea, and seven suites, such as the VIP (above), all of which mix antiques with contemporary design. The atmosphere is relaxed, especially in the oriental-style candlelit pool bar and restaurant.
11 Litous, Vouliagmeni, T 210 892 9000, www.themargi.gr

Semiramis

When flamboyant designer Karim Rashid was commissioned to transform Semiramis into Athens' first 'design' hotel, everyone expected it to be innovative and radical. It was. There are 51 spacious rooms in all, 42 Superiors with a park or pool view, five Bungalows set around a gorgeous shoehorn-shaped pool (overleaf), three Penthouse Studios and one Penthouse Suite (above), which offers a wonderful view of the city, filtered through ultra-modern pop aesthetics. A colour explosion (pinks, greens and yellows), innovative lighting and unique furniture all reflect the designer's playful style.
48 Charilaou Trikoupi, T 210 628 4400, www.semiramisathens.com

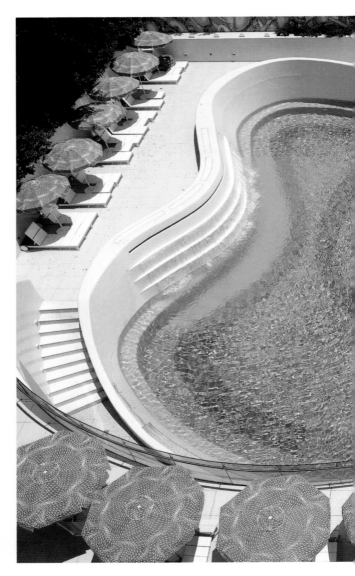

Pool, Semiramis

24 HOURS

SEE THE BEST OF THE CITY IN JUST ONE DAY

It might be a tight schedule, but it is possible to capture the essence of Greece's multifaceted culture in a single day. You must not miss the relics of antiquity; add touches of Christianity by visiting a historic Byzantine church, such as the Agios Nicolaos Rangavas (1 Pritaniou). The Athens Sightseeing Public Bus (Line 400) will take you to 20 attractions, including the Archaeological Museum (44 Patission, T 210 821 7717) and the National Gallery (50 Vasileos Konstantinou, T 210 723 5857). When it comes to modern art, although the Greek capital is far from being a major player in the international art arena, the Athens Biennial (www.athensbiennial. org), to be held in September 2007, will be of interest.

After all this food for the soul, you'll need real sustenance too. Sample a traditional cheese or aubergine pie in Ariston (10 Voulis, T 210 322 7626) and call in at a Greek taverna, such as Oikonomou (see p045). Later on, replace the local spirit with a global one by checking out the city's bar and club scene. The multifunctional building Bios (81 Pireos, T 210 342 5335) offers live music or DJ sets, as well as art, cinema and theatre. Soul (65 Evripidou, T 210 331 0907) has an unpretentious atmosphere, with a small, high-spirited club upstairs and a hip courtyard in summer. If you're in Psyrri at first light, grab a sugary doughnut or a *koulouri* (sesame-topped round bread); the bakery on Karaiskaki is a good bet.
For full addresses, see Resources.

10.00 Gallery Café

Greeks don't usually eat breakfast, they just have coffee (local or otherwise), so grab a bite at your hotel and then follow the local ritual: buy a newspaper from a kiosk in Syntagma Square and take a dose of caffeine at one of the plentiful cafés on Adhrianou (which joins Monastiraki to Thissio), overlooking the Ancient Agora. The best spot is in the colourful Gallery Café, located in front of Attalos Arcade.

The stone walls are lined with paintings and interesting sculptural pieces are dotted about. There's a great atmosphere and the coffee is very good. Afterwards, pretend to be a peripatetic philosopher as you pass by the ancient Athenian citizens buried in Keramikos cemetery. *33 Adhrianou, T 210 324 9080*

13.00 Mpakaliko Ola Ta Kala

Simple Greek and Mediterranean dishes, along with large, healthy salads and irresistible desserts, are served up in this deli/restaurant that specialises in Greek products. Mpakaliko, meaning old-style mini-market, has its own modern way of treating tradition: dressing it up smartly. With a friendly attitude and a functional design style, this is foodie heaven. Small suppliers from around the country provide a large selection of local cheeses, olives, sauces and handmade pasta to the two branches (there's also one in Glyfada, T 210 898 1501), as well as rare Greek delicacies. *238-240 Kifissias, T 210 808 9908*

16.00 DESTE

For a dose of culture, head to DESTE, the Foundation for Contemporary Art, in the suburb of New Ionia. It's a non-profit organisation that explores trends in contemporary art and culture through exhibitions and publications. Established by renowned collector Dakis Ioannou in 1983, DESTE brings major artists from around the world a bit closer to Athenian art lovers, while introducing Greek art to an international audience. The latter is further promoted by the DESTE Prize, awarded every two years to a Greek artist. *11 Filellinon/Emanouel Pappa, T 210 275 8490, www.deste.gr*

19.00 The Breeder

Founded in 2002 by George Vamvakidis, Stathis Panagoulis and Natasha Adamou, The Breeder has an experimental aura, inviting in foreign curators and showing both emerging artists and established names, local and international. It focuses on young talent, aged from 22 to 30, a strategy that seems to be working just fine. This is also one of the few Greek galleries that takes part in global art fairs, such as Liste in Basel, The Armory Show in New York, Art Basel Miami Beach and London's Frieze Art Fair. The Breeder's commitment to a diversity of subjects and artists, including Vangelis Vlahos, Jannis Varelas, Marc Bijl and Marcus Amm, makes it a worthwhile destination for any contemporary art fan. *6 Evmorphopoulou, T 210 331 7527, www.thebreedersystem.com*

22.00 Oikonomou

You really shouldn't leave Athens without experiencing a genuine Greek taverna. Authentic, traditional dishes, home-style cooking and a hospitable atmosphere are all to be found at Oikonomou. The décor is reminiscent of eateries of the 1950s and 1960s, especially the antiquated fridge, which is, amazingly, still working, and the casserole dishes and saucepans used in the kitchen. Order the lamb fricassee with lettuce, the very popular rabbit stew, and some delicious aubergines and artichokes; even the beans taste terrific here. Also try some local wine and a Greek dessert.
41 Troon/Kidantidon, T 210 684 4635

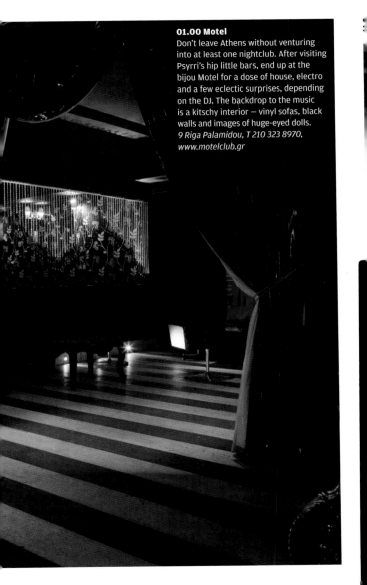

01.00 Motel

Don't leave Athens without venturing into at least one nightclub. After visiting Psyrri's hip little bars, end up at the bijou Motel for a dose of house, electro and a few eclectic surprises, depending on the DJ. The backdrop to the music is a kitschy interior — vinyl sofas, black walls and images of huge-eyed dolls.
9 Riga Palamidou, T 210 323 8970, www.motelclub.gr

URBAN LIFE
CAFÉS, RESTAURANTS, BARS AND NIGHTCLUBS

Some say Athens is a city that never really sleeps, but its bars and clubs are mostly only packed at the weekends, when they're crammed until 5 or 6am, especially in Psyrri, Gazi and the coastal avenue in summer. Athenians usually go out late and don't make reservations for dinner until about 10.30pm. Afterwards, DJs play international sounds, but you can also find a lot of Greek bouzouki (local music from the east) as well as belly dancing.

The cuisine on offer ranges from Greece's contribution to junk food, *souvlaki* (pork in pitta with tomato, tzatziki and garlic), to haute cuisine. Traditional tavernas, such as Skoufias (50 Vasiliou Megalou, T 210 341 2252) are as popular as ever, but contemporary versions, of which the best are Mamacas (41 Persephonis, T 210 346 4984) and seafood eaterie Piperia (8 Aggelou Sikelianou, T 210 672 9114), are more interesting as they're willing to take culinary risks.

Overall, Athens' restaurant scene is diversifying, with a variety of ethnic choices, such as sushi at Kiku (12 Dimokritou, T 210 364 7033) and curries at Red Indian (25 Epikourou, T 210 321 9908), appearing, but at the same time Greek cuisine is evolving. The international training of chefs has helped bring in some exciting ideas, and this reinvention of many classic dishes has resulted in some very good, innovative cuisine. A word of warning: even now, credit cards are not accepted everywhere.

For full addresses, see Resources.

Baraonda

An arty party crowd of trendy thirty- and fortysomethings, who can be a little cliquey at times, cherishes this much talked-about space in Ampelokipoi for its high-energy music and cuisine. The restaurant is atmospheric, with stone and tiled walls, red velvet curtains and candles, but it's probably the adventurous if expensive Mediterranean menu that acts as the real magnet. The rest of the venue includes elegant drinking tables and armchairs, where you can lounge while ordering from an impressive list of wines and spirits. There are also a couple of bars and a private area, and in summer you can sit in the garden. But it's hard to resist the interior, where the ceiling opens and chandeliers appear to hang from the sky. It's a good idea to book in advance.
43 Tsoxa, T 210 644 4308

Aneton
Intimate and reasonably priced, this restaurant couples a modern interpretation of Greek cuisine with a stylish interior, featuring vintage furniture and a cute 'living room' area where you wait for your table. The kitchen is open, the staff are friendly and a planned 'glasshouse' out front should make it a great winter haunt.
19 Stratigou Lekka, T 210 806 6700

Spondi

Michelin-starred Spondi is the perfect choice for those who love haute cuisine touches (linen tablecloths, Riedel crystal, an excellent wine list and impeccable service). There is a beautiful courtyard and terrace open in the summer, and an attractive setting inside; the space is divided into different rooms, with stone walls covered in modern artwork. Or you may prefer the vaulted stone cellar. The menu here offers modern takes on French bourgeois classics, with the addition of Mediterranean flavours. Dishes bear the signature of consultant chef Eric Frechon, and the cooking is spot on.

5 Pyrronos, T 210 752 0658, www.spondi.gr

Cosa Nostra

This could be a part of New York's Little Italy that got tired of Manhattan and relocated to the centre of Athens. Cosa Nostra seems like a regular Italian joint from the outside, but the interior is more *Sopranos* than *Shirley Valentine*: there are pictures of proud Mafia families covering the walls, liquor boxes dating from the Prohibition era and a vintage jukebox providing the music. Even the restroom is an old barber's shop, fully equipped. Cosa Nostra's menu consists mainly, as you might expect, of familiar Italian classics. If you like pasta, wine and a convivial setting, this is the place for you.
5 Aghias Theklas, T 210 331 0900

Mommy
This venue takes its food and drink
seriously enough, but you won't be
guaranteed a quiet dinner at Mommy,
thanks to its resident DJs. The menu
draws on Mediterranean cuisine, the
surroundings are colourful, and include
regular contemporary art exhibitions
and the atmosphere is clubby.
*4 Delphon, T 210 361 9682,
www.mommy.gr*

Oil Resto

Hidden away in the district of Ilion, Oil Resto has two faces. In winter, you can sit in the small, simply decorated interior, where warm lighting creates a cosy feel. In summer, you have the choice of a luscious garden, a less hip but more natural environment. Best of all, though, is the food itself. The two young chefs improvise on modern Greek cuisine, while Oil Resto's owners Nick Kallergi and Nick

Boubas produce their own olive oil, which helps explain the restaurant's name. The result is a rather playful menu made up of adventurous dishes with a modern twist.
93 Idomeneos, T 210 269 3230

Brothel

Dark but welcoming, this elegant bar/
restaurant, with its suggestively louche
name, offers well-prepared Mediterranean
dishes, such as shrimps with saffron, hot
potato salad with a fig sauce, and pork
with champagne sauce, served on velvet
sous-plats. Moulin Rouge-like lights,
chandeliers and retro touches are set
against a modern interior to create a
suitably slinky environment and cabaret
ambience. To get you in the right mood,
Brothel's DJs mix atmospheric sounds
and contemporary rhythms every night.
Orpheos/Dekeleon, T 210 347 0505

Varoulko
Since winning a Michelin star for its imaginative and artistically presented fish dishes, Varoulko has moved to a new location in the city centre, adding a modern slant to its décor. There is no menu to speak of (and no meat on the menu); instead you take your pick from the day's specials, which are exquisite.
80 Pireos, T 210 522 8400,
www.varoulko.gr

Nixon

Housed in a former warehouse, Nixon
is divided into a working cinema of 58
seats (actually velvety sofas) and a two-
level bar-restaurant, with wooden tables,
leather sofas and a wonderfully retro
rectangular chandelier, all designed by
local architects Doxiadis+. The food is
unexciting– it's pasta and burgers on the
menu – but it's for the bar that you visit
Nixon: two *Life* magazine covers dating
back to 1967-1968 and a picture of the
former US president during a bowling
game act as a reminder of the somewhat
incongruous theme here. Inevitably, the
toilet is named Watergate.
61b Agisilaou, T 210 346 2077,
www.nixon.gr

Bar Guru Bar

This lively bar/restaurant spread over the ground and first floor is located in a multicultural neighbourhood. The menu features Thai dishes, which are served up in kitschy oriental surroundings. Vintage pin-ups are hung on floral wallpaper, and huge Chinese lanterns are suspended above the bar. DJs mix up disco, rock, reggae and funk sounds every night, and there's a jazz club on the second floor, which hosts live performances by Greek and international artists; the mood is a little more sultry up here and the lychee martinis are excellent.

10 Theatrou Square, T 210 324 6530, www.bargurubar.gr

48 The Restaurant
At 48, gastronomy is pared with sleek
minimalism. The chef creates traditional
Greek dishes with a contemporary twist,
including truffle and sea urchin versions
of its famous *peinirli* (pastry), served
in an impressive space with white-leather
seating and atmospheric lighting by
Arnold Chan. Sit at the bar for tapas.
48 Armatolon/Klefton, T 210 641 1082,
www.48therestaurant.com

Galaxy

This rooftop bar and barbecue in the Hilton is definitely worth the climb. The highlight, of course, is the striking view, either from the open-air terrace or through the plate-glass windows. The interior is contemporary and minimalist, featuring decking and marble pillars. The charming urban panorama and starry sky are complemented by cool music that allows for conversation (something of a rarity in Athens), smart Greek and Mediterranean appetisers, a summer barbecue grilling fresh fish, and a vast selection of cocktails, which are served in stylish angled glasses that can prove a little disconcerting. Galaxy also boasts an encyclopaedic whisky and vodka list, although all come at a price.

Hilton, 46 Vasilissis Sofias, T 210 728 1000, www.hilton.co.uk/athens

Bacaro
Philippe Starck chairs and Pallucco
and Foscarini lamps spice up this ultra-
modern café/restaurant with its own
art gallery. Order a prosecco cocktail
at the bar or in the courtyard while you
admire the art, which is not just visible
in the gallery but everywhere, through
projections, performances and concerts.
1 Sophokleous, T 210 321 1882,
www.bacaro.gr

Pisina
The name (Greek for swimming pool) no doubt gives you a picture of this spacious café/restaurant. By day, Pisina is a great escape from the summer heat – sip an iced coffee by the pool, overlooking the yachts lined up in the marina. At night, drink a cocktail by the candlelit water, ordering from the small selection of Mediterranean dishes on the menu. The interior is sleekly modern, with amazing lamps reminiscent of *A Clockwork Orange* aesthetics and comfy sofas for you to dive into when the pool is not in use.
Marina Zeas, T 210 451 1324,
www.pisinacafe.gr

INSIDERS' GUIDE
GREECE IS FOR LOVERS, PRODUCT DESIGNERS

Vasso Damkou, Thanos Karampatsos and Christina Kotsilelou, or Greece Is For Lovers (13a Karyatidon, T 210 924 5064) as they're collectively known, are three designers who comment on Greek habits and customs. Their ceramic ashtray-pot, for example, is inspired by the fact that smokers extinguish their cigarettes in flowerpots. The trio have added traditional dance-step motifs to curtains and created a bikini wine cooler, ideal for the beach.

When not playing with materials and ideas, they'll visit Varsos in Kifissia (5 Kassaveti, T 210 801 2472) to enjoy some milk or rice pudding in a 1950s setting, or order espressos in the minimalist Danesi Caffé (37 Skoufa, T 210 361 3823). They like cocktails at the Polynesian Kona Kai Restaurant in the Ledra Marriott Hotel (115 Syngrou, T 210 930 0074) and eat sushi as they view the Acropolis from the roof at Kyoto (5 Garivaldi, T 210 924 1406). The darkish, old-fashioned Vrettos (41 Kydathinaion) or Au Revoir (136 Patision, T 210 822 3966) are favourite haunts for drinks.

When it comes to shops, they head to Parthenis (20 Dimokritou/ Tsakalof, T 210 363 3158) for its simple lines, and ED Alexandrakis (27 Ermou, T 210 323 3262) for Pringle and John Smedley. For one-off pieces, Greece Is For Lovers recommends Mohnblumchen (Dexamenis Square, T 210 723 6960) and the striking art-jewellery at Andronikos Sagiannos (3 Makrigianni, T 210 924 7323).

For full addresses, see Resources.

ARCHITOUR

A GUIDE TO THE CITY'S ICONIC BUILDINGS

Like other cities without an urban plan, Athens – its ancient part excepted – is a tight structure lacking obvious character, having undergone an uncontrollable metamorphosis in a climate of little architectural integrity. A dire housing shortage led to a glut of basic apartment blocks (plain boxes, really) that devoured earlier residencies until the mid 1960s – a loss that was not acknowledged until many years later. Smaller-scale residential developments in the suburbs did something to compensate, with more adventurous constructions and restored 19th-century neoclassical buildings. And then came the office blocks (usually curtains of glass over an aluminium framework), cinema multiplexes, malls, a metro line and sports venues transformed for the 2004 Olympics.

This is not to say that Athens is without modern architectural merit. The renovated historic Pallas Theatre (1 Voukourestiou, T 210 331 7931) hosts music and dance productions, and is the most interesting newcomer. The former Fix Brewery, a vast international style building designed by Takis Zenetos and Margaritis Apostolidis in 1957, is due to be transformed into the National Museum for Contemporary Art (Syngrou/Frantzi, T 210 924 2111). The long-awaited New Acropolis Museum (Dhionysiou Areopayitou), designed by Bernard Tschumi and Michael Photiadis, incorporates an archaeological excavation site on its ground level.

For full addresses, see Resources.

Hellenic Cosmos Cultural Centre

This non-profit institution pays homage to Greek history and tradition through technology. Interactive multimedia exhibitions and 3D screenings make an impressive way to travel back in time. Architects Giorgos Andreadis, Natalia Efremoglou and Marina Dede converted part of this 1940s factory complex into an exhibition hall and various public spaces, each with its own defined use.

The ribbed dome (*tholos* in Greek), a high-tech reinterpretation of Bronze Age beehive tombs, houses a virtual-reality tour of ancient Hellenic culture.
254 Pireos, T 210 483 5300, www.fhw.gr

Kotzia Square

Syntagma Square and Omonia Square are more famous, but visit Kotzia too. Athens City Hall, designed by Panagis Kalkos in 1874, is a fine example of neoclassical architecture in the heart of the historic centre. After restoration, it once more became the seat of the municipal authority. Inside, frescoes by Giorgos Gounaropoulos and Fotis Kontoglou relate the city's history. Walk along Athinas Street at night to take in the beautiful scenery. Here, neoclassicism, mostly eliminated in Athens by brutalist apartment blocks, strikes a blow back with the newly refurbished National Bank of Greece Cultural Centre (T 210 323 0900). Just a little further away is the geometric modernism of the National Bank of Greece Administration Building (2001), designed by Swiss architect Mario Botta.

Pireos street graffiti

The Doric Temple of Hephaestus, built in 449BC, is indisputably the main symbol of the Thission area. But there's a modern icon appearing nearby. The walls of the public trolley depot have been covered by graffiti created by celebrated Brazilians Os Gemeos (The Twins) and Greek aerosol kings Woozy, Same, the OFK Crew, Jasone, Live2 and Nade. You get a strong, warm feeling from this art, an initiative of the Carpe Diem graffiti group, supported by the City of Athens and General Secretary of Youth. Hephaestus, the blacksmith god, would probably approve of the section where a giant destroys cars.

Pireos, opposite Technopolis

Cultural Centre, Benaki Museum

The original Benaki Museum (T 210 367 1000), located at 1 Koumbari/Vasilissis Sofias, which was founded back in 1930, is neoclassical and houses a collection that ranges from the Neolithic period to the 20th century. This new Cultural Centre was adapted from a 1960s car factory showroom by architects Maria Kokkinou and Andreas Kourkoulas. The beautiful red box features a wooden slatted courtyard (pictured), where open-air concerts are held. As well as the exhibition halls and amphitheatre, there is also a gift shop selling inventive objects by local artists.
138 Pireos/Andronikou, T 210 345 3111, www.benaki.gr

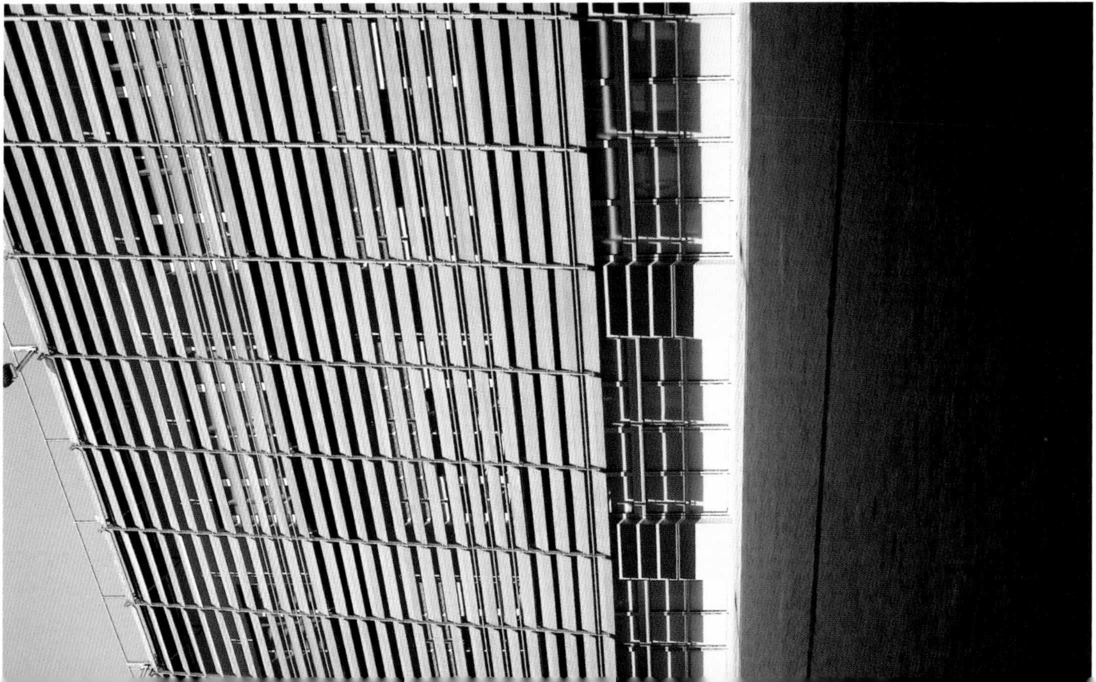

SHOPPING
THE BEST RETAIL THERAPY AND WHAT TO BUY

Start off your shopping trip in a leisurely way, wandering around the popular flea market in Monastiraki. Discover a variety of stalls and shops selling everything from clothes and shoes to furniture, jewellery and bric-a-brac – it's wonderful chaos. If you're looking for something more folkloric, head for nearby Plaka.

Now you've warmed up, hit the boutiques. Athens might not be Paris or Milan, but you can still buy Gucci and Prada. Find designer labels and more in Kolonaki, at Free Shop (50 Voukourestiou, T 210 364 1308) and Sotris (30 Anagnostopoulou, T 210 363 9281). At Bespoke Athens (15-17 Anagnostopoulou, T 210 364 5518), the Turkish tailor Ferruh Karakasli creates impeccable bespoke suits in Moxon fabrics. Nearby are Hermès (4 Stadhiou/Voukourestiou, T 210 323 3715) and Dolce & Gabbana (4 Stadhiou, T 210 335 6000). For Greek designs, don't miss Deux Hommes (18 Kanari, T 210 361 4155), Lak (10 Skoufa, T 210 628 3260) and Yiorgos Eleftheriades (13 Agion Anargiron, T 210 331 2622).

Further out, head for Glifada or Kifissia, and Valentino (19 Kassaveti, T 210 623 3402); for a broad retail sweep, Attica (City Link Complex, T 211 180 2500), Athens' upscale department store, is worth a visit. Foodies can pick up delicious Greek specialities at Pantopoleion Mesogeiakis Diatrofis (Sophokleous/Aristidhou, T 210 321 1925) and at Mesogaia (52 Nikis, T 210 322 9146).
For full addresses, see Resources.

Vinyl Microstore

This tiny shop, with its quirky interior, is frequented by the city's serious music lovers. The fluffy turquoise shelves display a wealth of indie, avant-garde and dance music on both vinyl and CD, including many imports (rarities can be sourced on request). There are distressed, retro sofas to relax on while you listen to the sounds on offer, and a collection of vintage radios and record players.

The store issues its own releases through Pop Art Records, hosts intermittent live performances, and even broadcasts over the internet as VM Radio.
34 Dhidhotou, T 210 361 4544, www.popart.gr

Lifestyle Death
This converted warehouse has become
a meeting point for Athens' fashionistas.
White walls bring out the details in
clothes by Eley Kishimoto, Bernhard
Willhelm, Jens Laugesen, Lady Soul and
Peter Jensen. Pass through the wooden
panels to peruse the vintage Levi's.
It's all rather elegantly messy.
30 Triptolemou, T 210 346 6055,
www.lifestyledeath.com

Wine Garage

More of a boutique than a full-blown cellar, this shop specialises in foreign wines, but also offers a small, though representative, selection of Greek vintages. The original Wine Garage (above) is in Kolonaki, and there's now a second branch in Ekali (T 210 813 6775). Both stores tempt you in with tastings, which mainly take place on Saturdays, and a sleek, industrial-style interior. Here, organised storage comes with purpose and character: each bottle gets its own hole, where it lies patiently waiting to be discovered.
25 Xenokratous, T 210 721 3175

Mofu

Mofu's owners Andreas Antoniou and
Dimitris Dimitriou met in New York,
and when they returned to Athens they
decided to share their sense of style
by opening a tiny retro interiors store.
The shop displays an amazing array of
vintage furniture and objects: chairs,
lights, wallpaper, ceramics, art and more.
The duo carefully collects interesting
pieces from Europe and the US, dating

as far back as the 1920s. We loved the late
1960s chairs from JFK Airport and the
round JVC TV, inspired by an astronaut's
helmet, hanging from the ceiling.
28 Sarri, T 210 3311 9220

Mastiha Shop

The shelves here are packed with products made with resin taken from the mastic tree (*mastiha* in Greek), which is highly aromatic and said to be beneficial for the health. The colourful boxes, some showing beautiful pictures of Chios Island, where the shrub is cultivated, are a lovely sight. Mastic is added to a range of foods, from Turkish delight to chocolate, toffee, feta cheese and even coffee, and all taste quite distinctive as a result. There are haircare and skincare products on offer too. *Panepistimiou/Kriezotou, T 210 363 2750, www.mastihashop.com*

Museum of Cycladic Art

First, get familiar with the white marble statuettes that date back to 2800BC and have inspired artists worldwide, including Giacometti and Henry Moore. The Cycladic civilisation plays the most important role in this museum, originally built to host the personal collection of Nicholas and Dolly Goulandris, but it has since expanded to include many more ancient Greek pieces. Have a coffee at the attractive museum café, before exploring the shop, where you'll find excellent copies of the figurines, miniature olive trees, ceramics, jewellery and silverware inspired by prehistoric art.
4 Neophytou Dhouka, T 210 722 8321

SPORTS AND SPAS
WORK OUT, CHILL OUT OR JUST WATCH

Noisy, fussy and sometimes tiring, Athens can be stressful, so you might need an antidote. Escape the traffic for a few hours and shed the mentality of a struggling urbanite by booking the right treatment: you can never have enough pampering or exercise. Activities range from jogging (try the paths on Lycabettus Hill or along Coastal Avenue), tennis, aerobics and Pilates, to less active options such as yoga, massage or a spa session; the Grand Resort Lagonissi (see p032) and the Grande Bretagne (see p034) both have excellent in-house spas.

During the hot summer months, be sure to take advantage of the sandy beaches of the southern suburbs, including Glifada, Vouliagmeni and Varkiza, or the north-eastern ones, such as Skhiniás and Porto Rafti. As well as swimming and sunbathing, you can sample a range of watersports: sailing, windsurfing and jet-skiing. For a round of golf, the Glyfada Golf Club (T 210 894 6820) has a beautiful course, and does not require membership. And, if you have time, explore Athens' serious sports terrain more extensively by visiting the new facilities built for the 2004 Games, especially the Olympic Athletic Centre at the OAKA complex in Maroussi (see p094), the Olympic Beach Volleyball Centre at Faliro (T 210 922 2137) and the 5,000-seater Goudi Olympic Hall (T 210 685 0200), situated at the foot of Mount Ymittos.
For full addresses, see Resources.

Piraeus Sailing Club

Founded in 1937, the Piraeus Sailing Club has its own strong sailing team, which regularly competes in various categories (Optimist, 420, 470, Finn, 49er, Lightning, Laser Radial, Laser Standard, Laser 4.7, Star). Since 1981, the club has also run a sailing school, offering tuition for sailors of all levels. After a course that includes 24 hours of theory and some 64 hours of hands-on sailing, even novices should feel confident enough to set sail on the Mediterranean – on a calm day at least.
Istioploikos Omilos, Microlimano, Pireas, T 210 417 7636, www.iop.gr

Divani Athens Spa & Thalasso Centre
This luxurious centre has a 225 sq m
pool, several saunas, exfoliation rooms,
Turkish baths and a gym. Try one of the
marine treatments, such as algotherapy
(seaweed application) or aromaceane
(marine mud and essential oils), and
finish with a sea-water hydromassage.
*Divani Apollon Palace & Spa, 10 Aghiou
Nikolaou/Iliou, Vouliagmeni,
T 210 891 1100, www.divanis.gr*

Athens Tennis Academy

Take advantage of the Olympic-standard facilities at Athens Tennis Academy, which boasts courts of bright blue Decoturf II, the playing surface used in the US Open. It's housed in the Olympic Tennis Centre, designed for the 2004 Games by British architect Richard Rees, which forms part of the OAKA sports complex at Maroussi, 9km to the north of Athens. Be warned that the courts are often pre-booked by students of the academy, so it's advisable to call ahead and make a court reservation.
Olympic Tennis Centre, Kifissias, Maroussi, T 210 685 7917, www.athenstennisacademy.gr

Athens Olympic Sports Complex
When a superstar architect flies in and
takes over a project, you should expect
stunning results. The glass and steel roof
of the 2004 Olympic Stadium, designed
by Santiago Calatrava, is an impressive
work that dominates the OAKA complex.
Now admired, it caused many complaints,
mostly about costs, at the time.
37 Kifissias, Maroussi, T 210 683 4060,
www.oaka.com.gr

ESCAPES

WHERE TO GO IF YOU WANT TO LEAVE TOWN

For lovers of antiquity who want to escape the city, the closest solution is Sounion, with its glorious white-marble Temple of Poseidon (opposite). If you have more time, head to Nafplion (see p100) for some more recent history; it's worth the trip for the dazzling view from the Venetian castle and the atmosphere of the old town alone. The picturesque, traditional Saronic islands are ideal for a short break, although bear in mind that they can get extremely crowded at the weekend. Choose between visiting the neoclassical buildings of nearby Poros and Aegina, where you will come across the ancient Temple of Aphaia, the beautiful stone mansions of Hydra and, if you are travelling in September, the Armata festivities in Spetses.

If want to do some further historical exploring, make your way to the archaeological site of Delphi, which is located about three hours north-west of Athens – in particular look out for the Temple of Apollo, the Altar of the Chians and the Theatre of the Sanctuary. During winter, you can go skiing on the slopes of Mount Parnassos, stopping off for some hot cocoa in the little town of Arachova.

And don't miss the beautiful ancient amphitheatre at Epidaurus, which was built in the late 4th century BC and is a two-hour drive from Athens. Every summer, the Epidaurus Festival held here presents memorable performances of classical drama in Greek. *For full addresses, see Resources.*

Sounion

Either take the bus from Pedion to Areos or drive east following the coastline, and about an hour later you will arrive at Sounion. The imposing Doric-style Temple of Poseidon (above) was built in the 5th century BC; a sunset viewed through its columns is magical. The tranquil and chic Grechotel Cape Sounio (T 229 206 9700, overleaf) is situated far from the centre of town, and occupies a privileged location between a pine-planted area and the sea. The seven residential villas of the Royal Hill, which are decorated in earth tones and each have their own private pool, are magnificent. You can also opt for one of Cape Sounio's elegant bungalows.

Nafplion

It will take you approximately two hours by car to reach Nafplion (left), the first capital of the modern Greek state. On arrival, take a deep breath and climb the 999 steps to Palamidi, a castle built during the Venetians' occupation, to admire the view of the Argolic Gulf and the fortified isle of Bourtzi. Later, take a stroll to the charming old town, visit the Peloponnesian Folklore Foundation

(T 275 202 8379), then The Art Shop on Ipsilandou (T 275 202 9546), which sells works by Greek and international artists. The Nafplia Palace hotel (T 275 207 0800, above), which was built between 1968 and 1980, is set within the ancient fortress of Akronafplia. Its retro-futuristic entrance (overleaf) was blasted through solid rock.

Nafplia Palace

NOTES

SKETCHES AND MEMOS

RESOURCES
CITY GUIDE DIRECTORY

HOTELS
ADDRESSES AND ROOM RATES

Astir Palace 019
  Arion Resort & Spa
  Room rates:
  double, from €450
  The Westin
  Room rates:
  double, €390; suite, €1,260;
  Ambassador Suite, €1,260
  40 Apollonos
  Vouliagmeni
  T 210 890 2000
  www.astir-palace.gr

Baby Grand 028
  Room rates:
  double, from €130;
  Deluxe Room, from €180;
  suite, from €230
  65 Athinas/Lykourgou
  T 210 325 0900
  www.grecotel.gr

Eridanus 016
  Room rates:
  double, €190;
  78 Pireos
  T 210 520 5360
  www.eridanus.gr

Fresh 022
  Room rates:
  double, €140;
  Executive Room, €200;
  Suite 707, €300
  26 Sophokleous/Klisthenous
  T 210 524 8511
  www.freshhotel.gr

Grande Bretagne 034
  Room rates:
  double, €600;
  suite, €960-€14,000;
  Royal Suite, €16,000
  Consitution Square
  T 210 333 0000
  www.grandebretagne.gr

Grand Resort Lagonissi 032
  Room rates:
  all on request
  40km Athens-Sounio
  Lagonissi
  T 229 107 6000
  www.grandresort.gr

Life Gallery 024
  Room rates:
  double, €690;
  Superior Room, €810
  103 Leoforos Thisseos
  T 210 626 0400
  www.bluegr.com

The Margi 036
  Room rates:
  double, from €180;
  suite, from €350;
  VIP Suite, from €1,150
  11 Litous
  Vouliagmeni
  T 210 892 9000
  www.themargi.gr

Ochre & Brown 018
  Room rates:
  double, €178-€210;
  Junior Suite, €300
  7 Leokoriou
  T 210 331 2950
  www.ochreandbrown.com

Pentelikon 016
  Room rates:
  double, €315
  66 Dheliyianni
  T 210 623 0650
  www.hotelpentelikon.gr
Periscope 026
  Room Rates:
  double, €150; Junior Suite, €260;
  Penthouse Suite, €400
  22 Haritos
  T 210 729 7200
  www.periscope.gr
St George Lycabettus Hotel 030
  Room rates:
  double, €253;
  Marie Cristine Suite, €1,115
  2 Kleomenous
  T 210 729 0711
  www.sglycabettus.gr
Semiramis 037
  Room rates:
  double, €275;
  Superior Room, €300;
  Bungalow, €400;
  Penthouse Studio, €450;
  Penthouse Suite, €650
  48 Charilaou Trikoupi
  T 210 628 4400
  www.semiramisathens.com
Twentyone 017
  Room rates:
  Superior Room, €270;
  Loft Suite, €365
  21 Kolokotroni/Mykonou
  T 210 623 3521
  www.twentyone.gr

WALLPAPER* CITY GUIDES

Editorial Director
Richard Cook

Art Director
Loran Stosskopf
City Editor
Angela Stamatiadou
Project Editor
Rachael Moloney
**Executive
Managing Editor**
Jessica Firmin

Chief Designer
Ben Blossom
Designer
Ingvild Sandal

Map Illustrator
Russell Bell

Photography Editor
Christopher Lands
Photography Assistant
Jasmine Labeau

Chief Sub-Editor
Jeremy Case
Sub-Editor
Stephen Patience
Assistant Sub-Editor
Milly Nolan

Intern
Caroline Peers

**Wallpaper* Group
Editor-in-Chief**
Jeremy Langmead
Creative Director
Tony Chambers
Publishing Director
Fiona Dent

Contributors
Paul Barnes
Jeroen Bergmans
Alan Fletcher
Sara Henrichs
David McKendrick
Stephen Patience
Claudia Perin
Meirion Pritchard
Ellie Stathaki

PHAIDON

Phaidon Press Limited
Regent's Wharf
All Saints Street
London N1 9PA

Phaidon Press Inc
180 Varick Street
New York, NY 10014
www.phaidon.com

First published 2007
© 2007 Phaidon
Press Limited

ISBN 978 0 7148 4730 6

A CIP Catalogue record
for this book is available
from the British Library.

All prices are correct at
time of going to press,
but are subject to change.

Printed in China

PHOTOGRAPHERS

Sue Barr
Nafplia Palace, pp102-103

Salvatore Vinci
Athens city view, inside
front cover
Technopolis, pp010-011
Zappeion Hall and
Gardens, p012
Athens Academy, p013
Panathenaic Stadium,
pp014-015
Twentyone, p017
Astir Palace, p019
The Westin, pp020-021
Life Gallery, p025
Periscope, p026, p027
Grand Resort Lagonissi,
p032, p033
Gallery Café, p041
Mpakaliko Ola Ta Kala,
p042
DESTE, p043
The Breeder, p044
Oikonomou, p045
Motel, pp046-047
Baraonda, p049
Aneton, pp050-051
Spondi, p052
Cosa Nostra, p053
Mommy, pp054-055
Oil Resto, p056

Brothel, p057
Varoulko, pp058-059
Nixon, p060
Bar Guru Bar, p061
48 The Restaurant,
pp062-063
Bacaro, pp066-067
Pisina, pp068-069
Greece Is For Lovers, p071
Hellenic Cosmos Cultural
Centre, p073
Kotzia Square, pp074-075
Pireos street graffiti,
pp076-077
Cultural Centre, Benaki
Museum, pp078-079
Vinyl Microstore, p081
Lifestyle Death,
pp082-083
Wine Garage, p084
Mofu, p085
Mastiha Shop, p086
Museum of Cycladic Art
Shop, p087
Piraeus Sailing Club, p089
Divani Athens Spa
& Thalasso Centre,
pp090-091
Athens Tennis Academy,
pp092-093
Athens Olympic Sports
Complex, pp094-095
Sounion, p097
Nafplion, p100

ATHENS

A COLOUR-CODED GUIDE TO THE HOT 'HOODS

PLAKA, THISSIO AND MONASTIRAKI
The ancient heart of the city is home to the Acropolis and other major historical sites

PSYRRI AND GAZI
A plethora of bars and clubs make this lively district the place to come for local nightlife

NORTHERN SUBURBS
This greener part of town oozes old-school glamour and boasts designer boutiques

SOUTHERN SUBURBS
Beaches, promenades and nightlife make the seafront neighbourhoods fun in summer

SYNTAGMA AND KOLONAKI
Come here for museums, embassies, neoclassical architecture and some chic shopping

PAGRATI AND AMPELOKIPOI
This district boasts a clutch of landmark buildings, from ancient Olympian to modernist

For a full description of each neighbourhood,
including the places you really must not miss, see the Introduction